this book belongs to:

_____

Midnight
Mushroom

Aurora Woods

Thank you for your purchase!

Please help others find our coloring books by writing a review or sharing your finished colored pages. All feedback is greatly appreciated.

How to leave an Amazon review

1. Go to Amazon
2. Search for *Aurora Woods coloring book*
3. Find this book
4. Click on the *write a customer review* button

Thanks again! We hope you enjoyed our coloirng book.

Made in the USA
Monee, IL
11 November 2023

46233918R00037